*Seyhan Erözçelik*

# ROSESTRIKES AND COFFEE GRINDS

translated by Murat Nemet-Nejat

Talisman House, Publishers
Greenfield • Massachusetts • 2010

Grateful acknowledgment is made for the generous support given to
the publication of this book by the Turkish Ministry of Culture.

Published in the United States of America by
Talisman House, Publishers
P.O. Box 896
Greenfield, Massachusetts 01302

Manufactured in the United States of America
Printed on acid-free paper

ISBN 10: 1-58498-073-7
ISBN 13: 978-1-58498-073-5

Coffee Grinds

"*In our house lilies, roses,*
*magnolias, jasmines are blooming, while you are reading fortunes,*
*while I am watching, while I am reading fortunes,*
*while you are watching.*"

1.


People hold hands... this one in front, the other by the feet, the other by
and by, a tower of people towards the sky.

Stretching towards the sky.

Trying to catch the flying fish, reach it,
to arrive at it.

(*You're* first, of course...)

People burning incense in the sky. One of them is holding the *fish* by the
hand. All together they are on a long journey, mixing with the *smoke*, and
becoming an object.

One single object unified by smoke, *that* one which turns many into one,
dense and propitious smoke.

The holders of feet are suddenly constructing themselves into a swing on
the sky.

Then, the rainbow has become a *bow* of folks.

Then, it's *shining*, swinging in the sky, watching those below them.

Three roads are opening from them, next to each other, all of them
opening towards the same place, the sky, emptiness. Pure, blessed
emptiness.

The blessed smoke is taking the form of a person. A *saint* who makes
decisions. (Both a saint and a human being. A saint when  he pleases, a
human being when he does…)

In the full moon of the coffee grinds, together they are spinning, onto that the grinds won't change them, *onto* that kismet can't be stopped.

Together. In the sky. Becoming a human rainbow.

This way the sky turns human, as the fortune teller pulls, pulling the thread...

(The same tower of folks, the tower which has turned into a rainbow of people, is also on the saucer.)

Also wearing the delicate clothing made of coffee grinds.

## 2.

Here, I've turned up *your* cup. (Because the grinds are a bit dried, your fortune has *set*.)

(In order for fortune to *set*, must we make coffee grinds wait? Whatever, let's look at the cup, see inside.)

A mountain. Flying to the sky. (As in all fortunes, is this mountain *an inner distress*? Shouldn't words, as moving targets, in fortunes also have various meanings? And couldn't unknown words enrich the interpretation, therefore a fortune?

The mountain is flying to the sky, continuing to fly, leaving its main mass of land behind. But also know that that block of mother land also will not remain where it was—are themselves blocks which will continue to fly. As big pieces, as small pieces they will fly to the sky, there forming a mountain.

Mountain, in the sky. Even though their densities are different, only clouds may sustain their existence as mass. If so, what's this mountain which has rediscovered itself doing here?

*You* can tell me that. But it seems you're emptying your insides. And this, in the tongue of *our* coffee grinds, means an easing up. (Easing up block by block. If it happened all at once, it'd be like an electro-shock. Because of that, this way is a good thing. Maybe also the pace has to do with your personality.)

With this passing of the mountain to the sky, as if you are also being reborn. Midway, between sky and earth. And as if with your rebirth a crescent is oozing out from your skirt and mowing the skirt of the mountain.

Along with a cat in silhouette and a pregnant pigeon (or is it malignant) flying to the sky.

Between sky and earth, or, seen another way, like the depths of the sea. Heavy, silent, or functioning among the noises of the depth of the sea, the migrating mountain, parcels of mountain, rocks, stones, the silhouette of the cat, the pregnant pigeon, *you* wearing a long gown, tiny fish, a crescent moon like the knife… you're in that sea.

Or seen from another angle…

The crescent is also on the saucer of the cup, in addition, exactly opposite the crescent inside the cup. Exactly like the reflection of a mirror, the right side on the left. The left, on the right, etc. (Or, to say more, the West in the east, the North south…)

According to looking in the mirror, hearts are on the right.

Does this alter anything, anything?

Opposite the crescent (the one in the saucer, that is crescent in the mirror) there is a *star*. (Like a flag[1], exactly!)

The crescent becoming a full moon, that star also will keep growing.

(Why the mountain is migrating to the sky is now crystal clear.)

Finito!

---

[1] The Turkish flag has a crescent with a star inside against a red field.

## 3.

Wearing a mask, you're mingling with a crowd. There, beasts and human beings together… A midget with wings, or a midget angel, is viewing everything…

Holding fish and birds. Casts them over the crowd. Birds are flying. Fish diving into people's eyes, trying to swim. The fins are tearing folk's irises. The flying birds are regurgitating balls of fire.

Birds are bad news, fish, bad news, the winged midget, or the midget angel, also bad news.

Don't *you* ever, donning your mask, lose yourself in the crowd. (These folks are *all* leaning sideways, in italics. Don't ever mix with them…)

People, exchanging souls, are pulling each others' strings, in the sky.

From a lit up distance a man like the wind is approaching. (He is not coming like the wind, that is, adverbially, he's the wind, standing straight, looking every way…)

He's dispersing the clouds, the birds, the fish, the balls of fire, the winged midget, or the midget angel…

And in your heart, also, a good hearted rooster is rising, is being born…

This fortune reads *exactly* like a fairy tale. *Exactly*.

4.

Your coffee grinds have seeped out, it's raining. Exactly, such a distressing day. Besides, apart from reading your fortune I want to talk of other things. Which is not possible in every fortune. Now, instead of your fortune I'd like to be strolling in Moda[1].

Wearing a long gown, you will dance. Like the Spanish, shawl drooping from your arm. Turning and turning. Everyone will look at you, you'll fascinate every one. (*Which* is what the fortune is *saying*.)

Then, a path will be opening before you. A wondrous path.

You'll inflate balloons, fly them.

A crow, no, a seahorse with the face of a crow, is pecking at your breast. (This isn't a bad thing!) So that it pecks at you more fully, you are opening your breast. Then, outside, the *you* standing beside you, is peering at you at length. Analyzing you.

You're chasing someone, by *leaps and bounds*. The balloon, in the air.

The three of you, the dancer, the peerer, the opener of the breast.

*Yes* even the singer. Still in your ankle long gown.

The day is dawning in the East. The crescent still *there*.

And there are still things I can not write about.

*Is that fair, is that fair!*

---

[1] Moda is a seaside resort place in Istanbul.

5.

This fortune is woven loosely, there was so much water left in the cup. (Even this weaving of fortune loosely, *finally*, how much freedom does it leave a human being!)

You're with various members of the tribe of beasts. (You being the only Adam's descendant among them, but doesn't this lead to another question? how much of a beast you are, how much a human being? Saying it in another way, what's the *expiration* date of the balance, or its absolute lack, between your passions and reason?)

Here, the beasts: a bull on its hind legs, a playful fox, like puppies, a cat its tail behind it standing up, another cat squeezing the thought-balloon above its head, a fat beaver, a marten costumed as a bird, an ostrich carrying a rider on its back, a sparrow flying and capturing seeds, a rooster with seven heads, dinosaurs flying, walking within the time and space dimensions of a creature metamorphosing itself from a cat to a person, containing within itself all seven aspects, details of this metamorphosis, like a dream... in the middle *you*. In the middle of them and above them, *spraying milk* on all of them. Above them, and leaning backwards against them spraying it over into their world. You're lying on the ground, leaning on your elbows you are thinking, and shaking your tail a little. (Because you're in touch with the animal world through your elbows, they also bestowed you a tail.) This looks very much like Alice, wandering in the wonderland.

Amazed at everything or ready to be amazed, childlike.

Not childlike, a child, a baby.

(A cat, one different from the others, has grabbed a bird by its wing. *And this is the last news of the fortune.*)

In the depths there is a fault-line. That is, an earth-quake.

And in the coffee grinds on the saucer there is an arsonist. This is the second person in the fortune.

There's a person in the saucer. A person in the cup.

*This fortune's out!*

# 6.

An immense letter M. In the shape of a Moon. Or, a moon in the shape of the letter M is lighting this cup. A person with one horn (not an *equine*) is weaving for *you*. What kind is it? Like the human heart, it is knitting sadness, sitting down, meticulously. Click click. Click click.

Did I say sadness? No despair, dis-repairing, like Penelope.

You're right behind the person with one horn. And there is someone behind you. Is it male or female, I do not know, etching writings on your back. There is a halo around your head. (Can writing be *etched*, well, this one is doing it?) Again, a noise, clicking away. (Like the mechanism inside cats. Or a spool...}

Further back a woman. From her head down, she is pouring down the moonlight. (This's the light coming from the moon above.) You're going up, opening up to the world. (The one without *sharp minarets!*) Rising, the moon is getting bigger, its light shining, a third eye is opening in her forehead, the corona is spinning.

There's a smaller moon meeting the moon above, the crescent. It's looking around. Joining its own extremities with the ends of a circle. That is, the circumference is being completed.

A confused, and as much as confused, an exciting, terrific fortune.

*You are in the hands of coffee grinds now. Coffee grinds in your hands.*

7.


There, a road to outside from the cup, already visible, before lifting it up.
That obvious.

O.K. To where?

A shard is peeling from you, what's unfolding on the road is it.

Two of you, sitting and talking, besides, you're reading
his fortune. Who is a smoker, sitting in front of you, he is listening. You
    are reading to him, reading,
reading, so intensely that from you to him,
and him to you, something is shuttling, shuttling something
between you two.

Three roads, the middle of which is a tributary
of the road outside from the cup, you are crossing seas.

The cloud in the air is a splinter.

Like a bird with a long beautiful tail to distances, under a crescent mooned
light, the crescent moon waning for the next full moon, a wide joyful road
    is starting
out of the mouth, that is, you are coming out and leaving.

O.K., to where?

Not that fast. Tossing your hair, you're also seeing off
someone, like old times precisely, with a handkerchief
in your hand, a kid next to you. But like
seeing off someone sailing on a boat.

Someone leaning on your breast. Who that one is isn't visible, isn't legible. He's holding the star in his hand.

Your fate's in that star.

Then a rooster. A new rooster, cockadoodledooing in the moonlight. Ushering good news. A kismet, which will please you. And a cat also is letting itself be caressed.

Every coffee grind is you.

Which are endless.[1]

Pouring what was left on the saucer back in the cup, a new fortune.

The grinds are reforming themselves.

Whichever way I may play with the cup, I can't change your kismet.

That's the way the cookie crumbles...

(Ill fate, well made.)

---

[1] *Every coffee grind is you./Which are endless*: Like coffee grinds themselves, fate is splintered into different words: coffee grinds, fortune, luck, kismet, rooster, dolphin, cat, fox. One can see in this language its animistic, Central Asian origins.

Fate as a unifying concept is not spelled out, but referred to obliquely in its different manifestations, an unnamed core around which the coffee grinds weave their infinite pattern.

8.


A mass of coffee grinds's flying to the sky. A profound sadness is getting up,
about to get up, and leave, leaving behind its space
empty, that is, nothing to interpret
in its stead. Either for good or evil.

A portion of universe waiting to be filled, is what's left.

Something has ended, you're relieved, have gotten rid of a burden.
(What the load is, I can't tell.)

Inside the cup further back, a dolphin. The greatest of luck,
the most propitious object. Both a fish, and with lungs. Besides...

It'll drag you with itself, to the sea.

To the sea or the sky? If sky, is freedom, sea is mother's lap.

To the sea or sky? Various cats and roosters are also dragged with you.
You're on the road on a royal progress, together, towards somewhere.
Two roosters, one cat and the fish.

The dolphin leading the way, a lucky and fortunate road.

(An event, clearly, affecting the whole family, by the way, good luck.)

That's what is beyond the emptiness. Something happened,
you are freed. This is affecting a lot of people near you,
along with you.

Affecting well and good.

A good reading. Wonderful.

Well, that's it.

9.

You are stretching for a fish. Fish, that is kismet, watch out... the Holy
Dolphin!

Two people obstructing you. Holding the tail of the fish, they don't let go.

Kismet isn't only fish, there's also a rooster flying
over the fish. Nothing is preventing it from
reaching you, but it's better if you can obtain the fish first.

Besides the rooster is a lesser kismet than the fish.

(Interpret kismet as money, luck, ease of heart, a swoon of heart, however
you wish.)

You'll experience a minor distress, but it'll easily go away.

There are two roads before you, directly relating to you. Because of that
you'll be forced to make a decision. And you must make it soon
and fast.

Depending on it, you can reach the fish, that is, going back,
if you choose one of the roads, a fish will appear before you.
(In this case, the idea of obstruction
is an issue. Choosing the other road,
there is neither a fish nor those holding it
by its tail.)

Coffee grinds in your saucer also, exactly in the middle divide in two.

Or two opposing but equal forces, coming face to face.

Which shows how hard it will be for you to decide which road to choose.

But decide you must, which you will.

That's it, I guess.

More, please.

Wow!
Don't ask for more.

# 10.

Your fortune has set like the Black Sea. Untrustworthy and heavy. Let's
read.

To connive something against you, djinns are holding hands, hand in
hand, have reached a decision about you. It's such a chaotic meeting that
the whole place is a mess. Sky and earth one.

You must consider, who, what these djinns might be.

Review acquaintances, relatives, when I say relative, I'm also including
your mother.

Reach a decision.

This decision is on your heart, and is above your heart.

You'll attend an important meeting.

(Here light, the Aegean light, is piercing through the cup,
with things I don't see. I never figured cups occasionally
could be translucent. Fortune tellers also it seems
may have inauspicious days.)

In this council, be firm. They'll try
to wheedle something out of your mouth.

Do I need to tell you that your heart is fluttering? Don't hearts
flutter inside all coffee grinds?

Yes, but why is yours fluttering a bit differently?

Didn't I just mention that djinns were stomping above your head, well these djinns are discussing this flutter.

In other words, something major going on. (The Aegean light doesn't let me see it, besides, one's fortune is illegible over water.)

Behind the swelling heart the horizon is tracing itself. (And it is vast. Is the tracing boundless, or the horizon, decide for yourself.)

I'll get to the point. There is a sudden danger before you.

Handle it... if you can.

No roads in the near future either.

You'll pray, did you ever imagine it? Believing that God exists in some shape, language, within the rules of a religion, you'll  pray.

Prayer, and a vow.

The coffee grinds are mixed. The Black Sea has flown, and ended. This reading has ended.

(In truth more... things under.)

# 11.

Lifting the cup up, almost all the coffee grinds slid to the saucer.

This is a sign that a great distress is soon, on the verge of being over. But you must give it a push also, to extract the distress out of you.

This sadness, this huge mass of coffee grinds has left waves of traces behind itself. But these traces can't be erased. Won't be erased.

Still, you'll start anew, an easy life. Like a bird your distress is flying and you're growing light. (Besides, what's left of the coffee grinds in the cup is so easy and open, that it can't be any better...)

I don't see any roads anywhere.

As for the saucer, there're two cats ready to snarl at each other. You want to rescue one, or to extricate him from the fight.

And the other?

Three, or four of you are going somewhere together. Holding happily hands.

Is that it?

That's how I read fortunes.

## 12.

Of course, this fortune is a little dry, unlooked at a long time
fortunes dry, dry and crack, like lands with no water.
Yet fortunes are fortunes. Still...

From the cup to the saucer, a big chunk of coffee grinds was falling.
That is, if I had opened the cup in time, read
the fortune in due time, that block'd have slid into the saucer.
Would have.

If I had opened.

I'd have read the slipping of that mass to the saucer as an easing, as a
    casting
out of some distress. But when fortune *freezes*,
I can't do such a reading. Because, I can't read
the fortune of the past. No one can. This way: I'm looking at *now*... at the
    *fortune*
of fortune.[1]

Think also this: between the time I wrote down
and you read this fortune, the rotation of the earth completed itself
a bit more, whatever.

-------

[1] Water is time, the mysterious catalyst in the fate of coffee grinds. What determines the fate of an arrangement, its reading? The drinker of coffee, the cadence and strength of the lips, as they sip the coffee, how far to the drains, how much liquid is left in the cup. The drinker then turns down the cup (like cutting a deck of cards). How long does the turned down cup lie fallow, the grinds trickling down along the sides of the cup. As water dries, the fortune sets; once set, they can only crumble.

  Then the reader interprets the coffee grinds.

  A coffee grind reading is a spirit echo of the world, consisting of the same four elements: earth, the coffee grinds; water, the liquid in which they move (time); wind, the voice of the reader; and fire, the urgent queries of the listener (also moon, his/her passion) which try to rush the dilatory rhythm of fortune, its telling.

(Whatever which is happening, twisting and going away...)

You gave birth to this distress. (Giving birth!) Consequently,
it has gained an existence outside, independent from you. (The distress!)
    There is
no cord between you two. O.K.,
giving birth to the distress, did you eject the placenta also,
I can't tell. Distress, to continue the analogy,
is fed by the placenta, finding sustenance, gaining its existence from it.

Did you start and go on a trip? You must tell me this part
yourself. (I told you, the inside of the coffee grinds has passed,
their time has passed.) But, if I'd looked at your cup in time
there'd have been a road. Yes, three roads. One towards the hills,
this you have to climb. One, towards the sky. You have, it appears,
to fly this one. Maybe you have done so. (Did you perhaps do it in your
    dream?)
The third, also towards the sky. But to the lands in the sky.

(Was looking at them, the coffee grinds crumbled. Of course, this is not
odd at all. I had a *déjà vu* , but didn't mention it.)

What else didn't I mention?

I didn't mention. (I see that the coffee grinds in the saucer have moulded.
    You know,
mold
saves lives. Wasn't penicillin discovered that way? Wasn't it?)

The fortune of this fortune. I snagged this one... let it be.

# 13.

Lifting the cup, the saucer lifted with it then fell. This act made a sound. Before being read, fortune made a sound. Is that understood?

The mass of coffee grinds in the cup is in motion. Luck, in motion. Kismet in motion.

To where?

Towards the inside of the cup. (When I say cup, you think I mean world, yours included... don't you?)

Fortune has stalled.

I'm looking. The moving mass of grinds looks like the *Nude of Maja*, reclining in bed, hands in her hair. But there is this difference: here she is mermaid. In other words: the *Mermaid Nude of Maja*. In an ether as comfortable as mother's womb, she is reclining.[1]

(This mermaid isn't you. But revealing of your spiritual state, both a child and a mother. Born and giving birth. That's how it is.)

A slight danger, a fish's trying to nibble pieces from this mermaid.

This danger will be averted, you won't even notice.

---

[1] Animal spirits populate the universe: cats, roosters, fish, dolphins, mountains (also infused with animal spirits), the sea, the sky, the crescent moon, all contained within the immensity of the arc of the horizon, which is also the dome of the coffee cup, which is the dome of the sky.

The coffee cup, the universe. The *fortune* of a specific arrangement, determined by a fusion of the drinker of the coffee and the reader of the grinds. Fate is a fusion of being and looking at that being; one reveals oneself by looking at others, using the universe as a mirror.

Wind and sea are into each other, with places beyond the sea.

Where to?

Due to the shape of the cup I guess, a horizon in the shape of a crescent moon is also in this fortune.

Everything is so clean, so peaceful.

But in the saucer, someone is carrying a gun. What it means, I couldn't make out. (That's the part of fortune which was still in motion.)

Fortune has stopped.

(Coffee grinds don't move any more.

What about kismet?)

14.


You are going to take flight, but to where?
First, your wings are big, so big that they are like the
sky. That is, in reality, they are the sky.
Then, as if, you are flying inside yourself.

The parcel of mass from the previous reading has fallen off. Is its place
now empty?

Not empty. See those wings made of sky?

There's the rooster. *Kismet.* Waiting for you, waiting to bring you news.

Two deer. Their antlers entangled together. Stretching to the sky, together.
(In other words, *to your wings.*) This is a kind of news also. This way your
inside will quiver, but it's a good quiver.

Someone older than you, with a beard, will keep handing you advice.
(Listen to him!).

You will dance with someone.

*This fortune is this long. A good length.*

## 15.

The great block in your soul has split. (Even if it is in like other fortunes, soul is soul, and block of soul, block of soul.)

You may interpret that splitting away as the relieving of some unease. But be careful. A *split away* piece of soul. Because the rest is *still* in the cup.

If everything'd gone, I could say you are at peace. But now, instead of doing so, with the rupture of the distress, the distress has increased. (That is the distress has splintered, a bit of it inside the cup, a bit on the saucer.) Now you have two distresses. As a result, the resistance you'll show each will be distinct.

*That way you'll feel powerless.*

*How much?*

The parcel of soul left inside… Until it un-snags from the cotton thread. That has something to do with love, someone who has grabbed your legs. *This*, you like! But, simultaneously, because of your *natura*, you don't like people grabbing your legs, hopeless, despairing people. (*I Wish he'd not grabbed your legs*!)

Yet, this doesn't prevent you from caressing his head lying on your knees.

That's why your distress! Why it's worse.

You're caught between two worlds.

All this will happen in front of people, in public. Maybe in a party. At that same place, you don't want to relinquish the hands of someone whose hand you are holding.

You are like a rock. (You know how there are boats hitting rocks in the sea?) But with this proviso that, you're a *swimming* rock. You may hit something too! (*What happens if you do so?*)

No news. No trip. No big catastrophe.

In the last dinner of the year, you'll discuss something with someone. You'll get *a bit* annoyed.

*Yet all these are only coffee grinds.*

# 16.

The rupture reoccurred, do you know? *Exactly the same!*

The fortune is breaking up like a fault. A break up of the soul. Soul's fault line. Earthquakes, as you should know, occur at fault lines. They contain, you *must know, aftershocks.*

Simonetta has not appeared this time. (Boticelli's...). There's no road, no catastrophe. There is no news.

The grinds left behind after the other grinds have left are returning, sliding back to the cup as it is turned up.

As I'm trying to realign your fortune, there is still a fault line.

Not setting. Or these coffee grinds are past their due date[1].

(Nothing's the same no more. That's, nothing could be the same. Among the grinds.)

Read the attached poem. (In truth, the words to a song.)

*A lie killed nobody! Nor a lyer!*

---

[1] In other words, the coffee grinds in the cup have become too dry, They are crumbling, instead of settling (which implies water's subtle movement) or setting (which implies form).
Every coffee grinds reading—of which there are twenty-four here—starts with a rejuvenation of hope, endless and ever changing.

ADDENDUM TO 16.

But I Am Still Sad

The past doesn't return, not possible, nothing here to mourn for.
Every age's a beauty of its own.
But I am still mourning, sad. *We won't be able to eat.*
With Alexander Sergeyevic, we wont be able to go to the friendly tavern
for two shots of drink.

No more is it necessary to grab things with your hands weaving down the
street.
Cars are ready, rockets are ready to fly us far away places.
And I'm still mourning sad, not even one troika left in Moscow
& never will there be any. How sad is *it*! isn't it?

O.K. I'm bending till the ground, my mind—wandering on shoreless seas—
honoring *our* empirical times,
but I'm still *still* sad. False idols are *still* false idols,
we are still *slaves*.

We were meticulous casting our victory,
*eureka, eureka*, we discovered everything. Harbors are safe now, and *here*
is light…
But I am still mourning, sad—the pedestal
of our victory is meaner, *steeper* than our victories.

The past doesn't return, *impossible*. I go out.
Suddenly before me Nikitskye Vorota.
*A troika is stopping*. Alexander Sergeyevic is going out for a stroll.
*Ah, maybe now something will happen.*

Bulat Okudjava

17.

Your fortune was sealed, with a ring on it.[1]

I pick it up, turning over the cup.

A big *rock fell* from inside the cup. A big weight fell, you feel lighter.

Boarding a cloud, you're flying towards the sky. Still ascending, a Japanese with an umbrella along with you.

Then you are tangled within the tail of a peacock.
Your *hairs*'s tangled within the tail of the peacock.

Someone, for you, is playing the flute. Stars are sparkling from the act, spreading to the sky.

The moon's born in it.

With a dolphin you are dancing before this moon. In the moonlight.

*And* on the saucer, there is still the moon. In a row, a moon, a bow, and an arrow. The bow's bent.

*The arrow's just flown, out of the cup.*

(*This ring has cooled this cup far too quickly.*)

---

[1] The person whose fortune is being told turns over the cup in the saucer after drinking the coffee, places his/her ring on it and waits. The grinds flow down inside the cup and dry. They are seeled/sealed.

18.

Even if the grinds were dry…

Flags, flags, flags…

The flags, carried by a convoy of sea horses, in the sky. In other words, sea horses in flight. Maybe, your heart… heart of hearts is born from these creatures, emerging from them…

Then, a dolphin keeps leaping in the sky… towards the flags. Towards the…

There's still the peacock. Its tail has become a net fronting the flags. In the sky.

The concave side of the cups, their insides, should they always be interpreted as sky, I wonder?

It's rain. You, with the parcel of cloud above you, are walking towards the flags. In the space of the sky where you are, there is no rain. But since there is a parcel of cloud above your head, you are always carrying the rain with you.

*Carrying where?*

To the tryst with the dolphin…

Somewhere behind you, in a very, very fertile spot, a large tree is standing. And among its branches there are *tiny tiny* fish…They keep gamboling, furling around.

*The sky's shaking, raining.*

## 19.

Let this one stay as it is—

# 20.

*(You'ere unable to settle your fortune. This is called coffee grinds anxiety.)*

The grinds have overflown the cup.

I'll start outside.

In other words outside the cup, there is an animal trying to escape inside, or trying to *enter* your fortune. Small, ferocious, beautiful hair… with a long tail. And the path before it wide open.

That *small*, ferocious beast has sent its *replica* inside. A replica of coffee grinds oscillating inside, keeps strolling, swinging its arms, as if it owned the place, in its own country.

A person without a face, holding a flag. (*The flag's appeared in your cup again!*)

Forest beasts, singing all together.

The swollen, bubbly places inside have stretched the coffee grinds like a membrane. If I say *piff!* It will burst.

*(Piff!)*

And the replica of the replica of the small beast also is in the cup.

Now inside the cup a universe apart, a separate world.
.
*That world*, expanding.

From the cup to the saucer a rivulet is running, a rivulet of grinds.

The beast of fortune, that very ferocious one, is drowning in this brook.

Reborn in the cup.

To put it in another way, it's jumped a threshold.

*To another world…*

21.

Fortune has dried again[1].

Let it. (The drying of fortunes show that fortunes *go faster* than our lives, it seems.)

At the bottom of the cup there is a *horizon line, water, sky, land…* all joining there, a guy has cast his tackle to the fish, is waiting. From above a strip of delicate road is descending directly towards him. Towards his thoughts.

Further back, there's a woman dancing, like the Spanish, holding waving a handkerchief. For whom is she *waving* it, why is she *waving* it, we can't tell.

A woman with wings, bending, is gathering something from the ground, some herbs. And why is she gathering them, *for whom*, we can't tell.

Another woman tossing her hair right and left is moving far away.

The crescent in the saucer has risen and *entangled* with her hair.

(*Then I touched the coffee grinds in the cup.*

*They are not dried. That's the truth!*)

We human beings, sometimes, pretend we don't know.

---

[1] The movements of time sometimes are much slower than the forward motion of our hopes— like paint drying, and our reading it.

22.


(The grinds are set. Ideal.)

Saying farewell to someone, you're going somewhere. There are saints
in this fortune, in this cup, waving after you. Somewhere you will go to,
and return. A propitious work. To resolve something. Well, go!

(Did I say saints? Nooo, fools!)

Wearing long coats. Like Cossacks. A giraffe is pulling your carriage, to
     near the hills,
near the sky, for a meeting.

(This is the fortune of a prophet! Very propitious, very!)

A shepherd's waiting for you. with full regalia, his flock,
his mild mannered dog. Like a gentleman he is waiting for you, greeting
     you
holding his crook.

(This fortune's like *The New Testament.* Till now no one could pull it off
and you did it. How did you... )

Two birds are dancing behind you.

You also are bringing a new book. Everything's pointing that.

The signs have disappeared now. *Beautiful!*

## 23.

It has set.
It *was* set.

*You* are clearly in your fortune,  and *you* are talking to someone. And the one you are talking to is like you a woman, with a delicate face—and she's younger than you. The cat and the chicken are listening to you both. But this is, somewhat, a different world—among the bestiary, you're two vulnerable human beings, one *old*, the other younger.

A bird is on your shoulder. That's good luck! A certain sum of money, a certain sum… but you need to be careful. A viper with a fox face is after the money. And the viper has a midget assistant. Hold on to it, it didn't grow on trees. It's halal.[1]

Have you ever had a pregnant cat? In confinement? It looks like it has given birth to new litter. It is nursing them. *In these* coffee grinds.

Two anxieties. Equal to each other… If they weren't equal, you'd have forgotten the lesser one, keeping busy with the larger, one anxiety makes one forget another. But these are equal... You're living them both, unable to shake off either. Or, it's like this: an anxiety has split into two parts. Let's call it the anxiety split. If anxiety is halved, it should disappear, shouldn't it? But that's not how it is. It doesn't end. The ending of anxieties depends on an arrival at the sky.

These still have roots on earth, and, because of that, before anything else, they must cut off all ties with earth.

Don't worry, it'll go away.

There will be a minor duel, and it will end.

---

[1] *Halal* is the Moslem word for Kosher, as in *halal* meat. As the word kosher, it also means legitimately earned, honest.

I'm waiting for the mass of coffee grinds to slide off from the saucer. It has not yet.

There is a ball of fire. Inside *your* inside. *And this is that kind of fortune.*

24.

The moment I turned it[1], a sun rose on the saucer. It's setting. No, it's rising. To be sure, *this also depends* when you are looking at this fortune. At this sun.

Outside the cup, there is the stain of your lipstick. (I couldn't read that part.)

What about the *inside the cup*? Unbelievable! Again, the sun is rising. No, it's setting. Whatever, it's horizon…

(Exactly on the reverse side of the lipstick outside the cup, rising, or setting, bright Venus or evening star—isn't it called Venus or the evening star, depending on when you look at it?)

At that time, precisely, three gentle natured dogs, evening or morning dogs, are going out for a walk, taking the mild mannered crow with them also. (What a *bunch*, isn't it, exactly like *The Musicians of Bremen!*). People are playing ahead games: quarreling, fighting wars.

There are five hills, all *these* occurring on the top of the highest one. (The hills are barren.)

Literally, dawn is pouring from the eyes of someone. This is the relationship of the people to each other in the cup: *Shakespearean tragedies with no murders in them*. Why do you look so gloomy, what's wrong?

In the horizon huge trees are growing. Dawn is pouring from their eyes.

---

[1] In other words, the reader removes the ring and the saucer covering the cup on which it lay, while the grounds set, and begins to read the fortune.

Milady,[1]


There was this cup. You remember? You drank your coffee; closed your cup for your fortune to be read. *Kapatmışsın.* While I was performing my routine tasks, you were standing over me, and asked me if I could read your fortune. I can't read fortunes, I said. Got work to do, I said. Well, you can read it later, you said. Fine, leave it there, I'll write it down for you when I have time, I said.

Great, you said, besides your hands are beautiful.

I looked at my hands then, to see what was beautiful about them...

I took one look and read my destiny in my palms. I was to write a book, it was written. But before I wrote that book, I would look at coffee grounds, it was written.

I was to read coffee fortunes. And write.

It was frightening.

A coffee fortune is to be read and interpreted only. Not written.
For once it is written, you become an oracle of some kind. Whereas the word, the spoken, evaporates into thin air. There can be no pledge.

Even if recorded audio-visually, it is invalid.

The written word, sign is what matters.

So this is how the book began. This is how it finished. You, are the reason.

I only read ladies' fortunes—ladies only. No matter what the level of my relationship with them was.

---

[1] This section is written in English by Seyhan Erözçelik himself.

On the other hand, they are our mothers. You too are a mother.

Never did I read a fortune again. I forgot.

Whenever my mother asked for her fortune to be read, I'd look away and whistle. All the while carrying within me the souls of Tom, Huck, Nemecsek, Holden, Kaspar and Riley. No more, no less.

*Ikra.*[1]

My desperation, Milady.

With all my heart,

Seyhan Erözçelik

---

[1] A word from *The Koran* meaning "read."

# Rosestrikes

"A poem, but a cry inside one word."

*"Because… I know in life why only lilies, roses, magnolias and jasmines open up, how they love me and what they find in me.*

*May be the blooming of a rose also is a kind of poem, I don't know!"*

# I. Rosestrikes

# Rosethroat

Magpie in my larynx,
marten in my heart...
females jump

i jump
right & left,
screaming
screaming...

but now I'm hoarse.
Rosedusts escaped to my throat.
A thorn pricked my heel...
At my most delicate spot

Magpie in my larynx,
marten in my heart...

I looked at the moon, hit at the heel
This pain has no relief.
No one likes the moonstruck...

if it's getting light.
That is, if it's getting light.

Now my larynx a magpie,
marten my heart,

rose petals pricked my veins.

While the marten's squinting
petals swim in my blood.

The marten's pumping blood to its thighs,
to my eyes.

And my heartflesh dry like a rose.

It's *beautiful rose*.

A fire in the rose.
Loves are burning.
Town is burning.

Roses don't look alike,
many, **many** more in me

Count  can't  endless  Insects

are touring my veins,
carrying dustrose to my heart.

All the roses are growing in my heart.
A love is burning,
no water.

I'm the fire  **itself**.
I grow bushes in me,
bushrose,
bushrose.

# Bushrose

I suck you.
The blushrose.

The wind blows, blows.

# Windrose

Twisted
round,
destroyrose.

Twisted
round,
back
squeezer.

Marten worships rose
sitting on my face,

Mattress turned
upside down.

# Cherryrose

I wipe roses on my lips.

I kiss your cherryrose lips.

Kissing, kissing so much...

my lips are cherryrose.

But your lips,
still taste of lips.

"Thanks!"

# Roseblood

My eyes caught a rose the whole night
round midnight, a needle on a rose,
to my eyes stuck, a potent liquid
is flowing from my eyes, as if roseblood...

# Moonrose

Moonrose!

My moonrose!

There,
withdraw your smile!

Amazing,
dust still
around the moon!

Here,
get hold of me.

# Thiefrose

The town is
burning the fire
in the rose.

O thou art
a thief!

A house fire
and a rose fire
are so different.

But my heart's
burning
inside the house.

O sweet thiefrose
I am sick.

Rape me.
With my invisible
groom.

In your crime
bed.

# Rosebelief

I don't believe in roses
because I am a rose.

Let it not turn left!

Left back,
it's crying.

Mountains—in between
pellets—
are falling
on its petals.

My heart in chains
looking at
mountain chains.

Am I a rose,
not  believing in roses?


*I've a mouth, but no tongue… nor*
*mouth or lips either…*

*If you do not kiss what good*
*are roses?*

*Let them fade,*
*I'm no believer.*

*You can't read a fortune*
*from its roses,*

*oh, no, I'm not a believer,*

*Just watch the moon beam…*

*She resembles the rose*
*it resembles the moon!*

# Litmusrose

Rose is a sensitive paper,
under eyes, under stance.

Blow on it, without smelling. Blow on it.
Quit smiling, blow!

Rose petals roasted are
touring inside the body
sublunary

My body's cooked but
I'm still a fire to you.

## Fortunerose

Fortune rains on salt marshes,

This is the condition of the rose. we sit up,
leaving behind coffee cups
to their own.

Leave tea leaves to their rose formation.

Through reeds the marshes refract fractions of the moon.

Passing myself
I pass out.

The moon rises.
The rose has left with you.

Gibberish
of the bursting heart
exiled
to alchemical
dots.

# II. Moody Love

# Birdrose

Sing
sing!

a bird
called

flying
prison

## Moody Love

In the rain
rose petals are shedding tears.

the leaves, drooping downwards,
are oblivious.

# Beerose

Before
sunrise
the moon buzzes
the darkness

bzzzzz…

The rose is paling
in jealousy.

# Constellationrose

Under
I'm silent.

The bush is growing
growing

the bush is opening
opening

the bush's in rose bloom
bloom

the rose is a bush
bush

insects are carrying dust
dust dust

roses are multiplying
multiplying

*I have complaints only against this one rose,*
*rose*

## Kinshiprose

Apple. Almond. Cherry. Sour cherry. Bramble, etc.

There is also pear and quince.

(Did I say quince? No, quench,
Heartless. A mouth.)

Quench,
it simply loves fruits.
Kin of the rose,
suitable to
quench.

(Still in love
with moth.)

oh, the bear's eating from trees bearing fruits!
from the thorn in bloom, the slowly melting dew

# Rosemountain

*The rose's leveling the mountain*

(squinting)

*even if the name remains Rosemountain.*

# Dreamrose

Last night the rose passed,
passed into itself.
I passed myself,
passing out.
Angels laughed at me
and passed.
it seems the devil
made a pass.
Rose petals passing
round my belly,
I freeze into **its**
solitude.
Aching nu cle ar pain!
The fire having fooled me,
hitting on me,
is fueling me.
A shiver!
The devil's passed.
But you, my love!
What about you?
*Lighting a rose's fire again,*
*you lit me up again.*

# Spin o sa

The rose is a movable mecca[1] spinning
the marten also
is spinning,
but the marten is agile a worker
on the skyscraper
of the soul cleaning
its windows.
loving vertigo, the marten
is spinning
agile and lonely
wiping
away. the rose is spinning,
at the *pit /*
*c h*
of the vertigo.

---

[1] Mecca is the fixed point in Islam, like Jerusalem, the light to which one turns during prayers. In Sufism, this fixed point is moveable, and that's why the disorientation, why its giddy, vertiginous ecstasy.

s-
pun
raccoon
worshipping
the rose

punished

the rose is a mecca
ablaze

whirling

the magnetism
is turning the raccoon
insane

the magnetism which is
rose magnetism

begging

to adjust
the raccoon's twisting its heart
upside down

and planting a kiss there

like the flag of an alien land
the rose
is turtling
in the heart.

blowing a fuse
words are morphing into toys… and start flying.

s-
*prung*

*the clock stopping*
*now…*

# Swimrose

Magnetism
swimmingly

the rose
swimmingly

the sky swimmingly
the green swimmingly

the clock swimmingly
i swimmingly

the cock
swimmingly

the clock
swimmingly

stopped
swimmingly

magnetism

swimmingly

# Threesomes

the moon rises
moonrose

i i love you
swoonrose

where where were you
windrose.

# H-Rose

the logs are cracking
in the heart

of my kitchen

               sparkles
of h.

The gibberish
of the bursting hearth

exiled

to alchemical

dots.

# Jamrose

Mom is plucking petals in the kitchen

Logs are crackling
pot gurgling
rose petals cooking

My blood sugar has fallen

My lips sticking

There's the shadow of the rose in the fire

Logs have cracked
pot boiled
rose petals cooked

My blood sugar's up

My mouth frothy

I'm in a coma and
… i don't remember

In a coma I saw mom
prepare


sweetjam

for me

# Rosecandy

I bury myself—
my cheeks are smudged

The moon rises against the rose,

stained,  gracefully.

# Revolverrose

i collapse

in your arms.

## Bluntrose

the rose turned out to be blunt
the heart to

S M I T H E R E E N S!

# Nailrose

everything
is slanted
towards you!

## Sand Pebbles

Our lips brush

here and there

*beware!*

I can't make it there

Come to me,

in me!

*aware!*

*where?*

*oh, where?*

# Acherose

The adoration lanced long ago
is still bleeding

# Frostrose

Meadow dream.

Ice
crushed
into steam

In sunlight.

A catastrophe.

In miniature.

# Dustrose

This storm
has elapsed, only a dust particle.
"*Whoof!*" if anyone says,
it passes,
any dust particle,

who knows to whose eyelashes,
eyesight?
(*because dust disturbs the eye*)
which dead rose,
which ghost rose?

(*I passed myself passing out!*)

dust is a mirage
inside the rose,

*elements dispersing too far… too far…*

rose is the mirage… the mirage
in the dust.

# The Death of Gestures

Dry roses on the table still,
I remembering who bought them
but not why.

Once—when I say once
I don't mean a long time ago, a few months—
we used to buy flowers. Us, all of us.
For every occasion, appropriately or not,
we used to buy them.
Once,
us, both of us

We wore out the roses.

But now, no buying. The time for roses
has passed. The wind has blown. Blown hard. Gestures are finished.
We lost ourselves.
and no more any one to give roses to.

Occasionally, we say this
to ourselves:
this is life, this is it,
we did this,
thus.
Where're we now?

And I say this
to myself:
I've spent all my gestures, no more left.
Gestures don't carry life.
One should measure out.
(*Two naked bodies*
*Belong in a bathtub*)

Besides,
i see the skull in my face
in the mirror.

Nothing can be same as before, any more!
We don't ferry to Üsküdar, either.

Even though...
though people need each other.
Why love together otherwise?

*To L.C.*


We returned each others' roses
to each other.
Yours's still in my *h eart-*
*h.*
mine,
in my hand.

my heel full of thorns.

leave
the rose with its leaves,
leave the leaves with their rose,
both smiling[1]

embracing

---

[1] In Turkish, "rose" and smile" are the same word: "gül."

Seyhan's ROSEBUD

KIRAÉI → the childhood of Seyhan

Hoar frost
to break
quenching → milk, mother's milk
white poison  THE PAST
countryside
(the web of countryside)
the name of a book (by Seyhan)

THE PAST

WHITENESS
CHILDHOOD = TABULA RASA

(Jake winter)

ROSEBUD → the childhood of Orson Welles
(winter)

KIRAĞI: HOARFROST
KIR AĞI: BREAK THE WEB/NET!
KIR: -COUNTRYSIDE
      -GREY
      -TO BREAK
AĞ:-NET, WEB, COBWEB
      -TO RISE TO THE SKY
AĞI: POISON

# III. Rosebud

# I. The Web

Dews are frozen. Therefore, a web breaker[1]
Frost bit into my heel,
wherefore, didn't I die?
Because frost is in my heart.
My soul is a website

When I was a kid, frost, crescently
sank into my heel,
mom said,
"it seems like the moon
frost sank into my heel."
Then, I died.
That is, as a kid, once...

Mom said.
I won't do it again.
said,
as a kid once I did.
I won't *die* again

---

[1] This poem (the totality of "Rosebud") is based entirely on the pun the Turkish word "kırağı," which means "frost" in Turkish. "Kırağı" is made up of the words "Kır," meaning meadow, and "ağı," meaning net (of). In other words, "frost" in Turkish is a "meadow-net," a verbal ideogram. "Kır" also means "to break" and "to hurt." The poem transforms this double-edged meaning buried in the word into a narrative of a young kid going out in the field early in the morning and crushing the frost with his heel, the thrill the act possesses but also the undefined trauma it implies. The title "Rosebud" points to the parallel between this poem and the Orson Welles movie, *Citizen Kane*, the revelatory moment in the snow with the sled the film ends with.
In Erözçelik's poem, a narrative based on a memory of childhood (Kane's secret moment of happiness with his mother) gets transformed into a narrative buried in a word, the ideogrammatic narrative the word contains.

That is, if death were
a *childhood disease*.

*Yet* stung into my heel
it seems once
I *did*,
hit hit by frost
in my heel.

*Then, then* into my heart.

## II. The Walk

"a brook hidden in lace…"


Frost is woven with straight lines, i.e., with alifs[1]
crossing each other. Manna pouring from above. Dust and frost
oppose, dust can't reach
the manna state without
a pour.

Alifs neutralize dust. On earth, where there is dust,
revealing a new pattern.

Alifs, aslant each other.

*Double double double crossing*

Sunrise—and cold—is the best place to see it.

The span of frost's life, crossing a kid's
gleeful heel (that is
my heel) or as long as the sun's heat.

Frost is alive within the moon,
pursuing its own pattern.

*Frost*!

A frog in the soul.

The daylight approaching, the kid steps on it.

---

[1] "Alif" is the Hebrew letter "*aleph*" in Arabic. In Arabic it is written as a diagonal slash disappearing two-thirds down. "Aleph" is also a symbol for the infinite in Georg Cantor's mathematics of transfinite sets.

The sky breaks down.

i'm in the web

The alifs turn to dust.

The alifs which cutting please my eyes spread to the ground
chasing me

Frost bitten,
I, his innocent face
in its most fiend tormented form.

Meadow crush.
A kid's rush.

## III. The Rush

The meadow walking kid. Stinging nettles are blooming in my heart.
A kid, as me, that is my heel, crushed
the frost. Fragments of frost broke the weave
in the heart, cut it
loose. Frost gone, only the cut endures,
colder than steel. The theft. The heel probed
the dust, inside it
looking for something,

But all is pale, forlorn frost!

(*I want to put my hook into your heart so that you can't unhook me.*)

## IV. The Crush

In the morning we faced a terrifying frost. Crushing frost and ice,
I saw
everyone else doing same.

As the rainbow pleases mankind,
so does, it seems, crushing frost.

Because the inside of frost is hollow, the sound it makes being crushed
is interesting.
(*Eureka*! Is that, in essence, Achilles' scream?)

As if a piece of music.
Exactly like the crushing of a particularly thin glass.
Maybe of a crystal bone.

If you haven't blown off already
forget this poem,
but not
*me*.

I
know
what youth
is.

*Treerose*

*Quince[1],*
*looking down*

*Apple (**hard**) heard*
*in a foreign language.*

*Apple of hurt lying*
*yellow bite on a foreign tongue,*

*releasing*

*releasing.*

---

[1] In the Middle Eastern mythology the tree in paradise is sometimes a quince tree, whereas in other places it is good only for cooking, releasing its aroma.

After a reading, the drinker of coffee "opens his or her heart" by placing the right thumb at the bottom of the cup and twisting it clockwise slightly. Does that mean that the wishes, hopes of the drinker, his or her dreams, and the reader —together— have affected the flow of fate —or merely revealed it— that twist of the thumb being a mere bravado gesture?

In Israel in 2007, a fortune teller was charged with "practicing magic," ironically the standard of proof of magic being the involvement of intentional fakery. The case was dropped because the court determined that there was no way of proving objectively what is fake or what is true in the human heart.

# A Reading of Seyhan Erözçelik's *Rosestrikes & Coffee Grinds*

## I. *Eda* — The Mirror

Seyhan Erözçelik's *Rosestrikes and Coffee Grinds* was published in 1997. It belongs to a group of poems published in the 1990's, very near to each other in time, pointing to a major change in Turkish Poetry. A few of these works include Enis Batur's "Passport" (*The Grey Divan*, 1990), Lale Müldür's "Waking to Constantinople" (*The Book of Series*, 1991), küçük İskender's *souljam* (1994), Ahmet Güntan's *Romeo and Romeo* (1995) and Sami Baydar's poetic output his first book, *The Gentlemen of the World*, published in 1987, to *flower world, published* in 1996.

Though each is very distinct and individual, these works possess common characteristics which place them under the rubric the *Poetry of Motion*. During the 20<sup>th</sup> century Turkish poetry created a body of poetry with unique sensibility and its own poetics. This poetics is called *Eda*[1]. One crucial element of *Eda* is its acute sensitivity to the historical moment and the location, in this case the city of Istanbul, in which it was written. It bends to them and is shaped by them. Instead of crafting political arguments, usually an *Eda* poem functions as a passive mirror, the experience of reading it being that of looking into a text which sheds light with dazzling clarity on the specific moment of the poem's own emergence and of the person reading it. It combines a historical condition and a spiritual response to it. It is attuned to the forces—often suppressed, tacit or below the surface—in the populace which are precipitating historical changes. It constitutes an implicit but potent commentary on them. The *Poetry of Motion* constitutes *Eda's* spiritual response to a pivotal historical moment in the 1990's.

The major movement that preceded the *Poetry of Motion* was the *Second New* whose major works were written from the early 1950's to 1970. During that period, Istanbul was a city of around one million people with a distinct

---

[1] To find out more about *Eda* and the *Poetry of Motion* see the essays "The Idea of A Book," the introduction to *Eda: An Anthology of Contemporary Turkish Poetry,* edited by Murat Nemet-Nejat (Talisman Books, 2004) and "Turkey's Mysterious Motions and Turkish Poetry" (*Daily Star*, 2004; *Translation Review,* 2005, http://www.ziyalan.com/marmara/murat_nemet_nejat4.h)

topological/psychic structure. Lying at the intersection of the Bosphorus and the Sea of Marara, it was split by an inlet, The Golden Horn, into two: the old city in the south which was once the site of old Byzantium and the capital of the Ottoman empire and Galata, the new city with crooked streets on a hill in the north. The latter was where the ethnic minorities— Greeks, Armenians, Jews—lived, and the fleshpots, the entertainment district of the city were located. Around this dichotomy, the *Second New* created a poetry based on a dialectic between official and subversive, open and secret, sanctioned and forbidden. A lot of the *Second New* poetry revolves around revelations, often of an erotic or political nature or both. (It sustains an implicit parallel between open and hidden places of the city and the revealed and hidden parts of a woman's body):

The overweening thrust of the *Second New* is expanding consciousness, in depth (revealing secrets) and range of emotions (expanding poetic styles).... *Pigeon English,* Süreya's first book, is a series of lyrics of seduction from the male point of view. What is amazing about them is the power dimension of the eroticism—love as a stripping of both the body and mystery. In spectacular image combinations, the poems implicate, seduce the reader into the act—keeping him or her grasping/gasping for objectivity. These image combinations are the great contribution of Süreya to Turkish poetry. They release the sado-masochistic, subversive side of Sufism into contemporary Turkish....

Ece Ayhan had to self-publish his first book, *Miss Kinar's Waters.* Instead of like Süreya's exuding a seductive masculine eroticism, Ayhan's book is opaque, personal, trying to hide, as much as to reveal.... All the poems are from the point of view of the victim, the weak, the powerless, including seduced children turned hustlers; many are gay. Even when the poem is from the angle of the seducer, e.g. in "Wall Street" ("Kambiyo"**),** the tone is elegiac. Eroticism is tinged with suppressed rage, which in flashes pierces through as implicit commentary. These flashes weave a melody whose emotional tone is lucid, transparent; but whose meaning eludes us, is veiled...

The pursuit of secrets is the metaphysical resonance driving the *Second New* poets..[1]


II. The Crisis of the City and the *Poetry of Motion*

From the 1960's onward Istanbul underwent a phenomenal expansion of population which, by the mid-1980's, had reached over twelve million. The poets of that over twenty-year period have difficulty adjusting to these changes. They continue to write a poetry based almost completely on imagery, following in the footsteps of the *Second New*. By the late 1980's and early 1990's, Turkish poetry—*Eda*—was at a moment of crisis. Outside rare, exceptional poems, Turkish poets were producing work that had little to do with the environment in which the work was being written. The poetry of the *Second New* depended on and reflected a relatively small city with clear demarcations, the ambiguous, evocative blur in its imagery implying secrets. By the mid-1990's, Galata (the heart of the *Second New*) and the old city had become a peripheral part of the city, the great majority of life having moved to northern suburbs, non-existent in the 1960's, or to the Asian side. The centrality of the Galata Bridge in the physical and mental traffic of the city, which connected the old city to Galata, was replaced by the two bridges over the Bosphorus connecting the European and Asian sides and which had not been built in the 1960's. By the 1990's, one of the quintessential qualities of *Eda* was missing from Turkish poetry: its intimate link with the physical and psychic reality its environment. It had become a poetry written about a city which did not exist.

Though the *Poetry of Motion* is the poetic response to this urban crisis, before its occurrence a historical event takes place:

… [In] the early 1990's Istanbul underwent a subtle conceptual transformation, in addition to its numerical one. With the fall of the Soviet Union, it became an economic and spiritual focal point as people converged from former satellite countries in the West and Turkish republics in the East, in search of goods and ideas formerly unavailable or suppressed in their countries. At this point, Istanbul

---

[1] *Eda*, pp. 13/6.

became transformed from a national city of twelve million to a global metropolis, a crossing point of conflicting dreams.

> ... [The *Poetry of Motion*] reflects this tectonic, strategic change.... In the new poetry the language *flattens* [italics my own]. The stylistic essence of the best poems of the 1990's is motion. Often written in long sinuous lines, in them the thought, the eye, the image never stay in one place, constantly shifting conceptual, ideological, or identity lines. The music of this motion across borders echoes Istanbul as the global city.

> In each poem, two seemingly irreconcilable concepts (or desires) are superimposed on each other, creating a flat, unified field. The poems reflect the impulse towards synthesis at the heart of [the *Poetry of Motion*].[1]

An essentially Eastern response to the 21st century, the *Poetry of Motion* is after syntheses. Echoing the Sufi belief that divine love reduces multiplicities into unity, conflicting forces in each poem are pulled together to create a field where psychic boundaries are eliminated, where the content of the poem turns into pure motion—free movements of thought/ light across limits. In this process, Turkish poetry crosses its own boundaries, reflecting the chaotic and rejuvenating forces released after the fall of the Soviet Union in the world:

> "In the poetry of the 1990's Istanbul changes from a physical place into an idea, an elusive there, a basically mystical, dream space of pure motion..."[2]

---

[1] "Turkey's Mysterious Motions and Turkish Poetry," *Translation Review,* 2005.
[2] *Eda,* p. 18

III. *Rosestrikes and Coffee Grinds*: The Split of Time

    *Rosestrikes and Coffee Grinds* is split into two, a before and an after. *Coffee Grinds* is the before. It consists of twenty-four fortune readings—sinuous, meandering, open-ended narratives of hope and anxiety, where the reader and the listener look at a coffee cup which has the shape of the sky. Together, they create a mirror across which are traced the fluid motions of desire, its expansive innocence before being dashed by the future. The grounds mixed with liquid create Rorschach tests spread at random over which, teasingly and cajoled by a listener, the eye spins its cadences of hope, magically transforming the materiality of solid and liquid into words—into light.

    *Rosestrikes*, the second part of the poem, is repetitive, minimalist, a poem of obsessive variations around the Islamic Sufi symbol, the rose. It is about the after—what has already happened—about loss. The poems depict states of disintegration where the consciousness is yearning for a state of union, the before. *"To L C.,"* for instance, is a farewell poem where loss (death, separation) and the memory of a once perfect physical union are superimposed on each other into one single moment:

*To L.C.*

We returned each others' roses
to each other.
Yours's still in my *h eart-*
*h.*
mine,
in my hand.

my heel full of thorns.

leave
the rose with its leaves,
leave the leaves with their rose,
both smiling[1]

---

[1] In Turkish, "rose" and smile" are the same word: "gül."

embracing

In Seyhan Erozçelik's *Rosestrikes and Coffee Grinds* two strands of Sufism are pulled together. One is the Central Asian shamanism from which its animistic impulse, unifying man's subjectivity and nature, derives. The other is the intellectual stricture, the bent Islam puts on this basically pagan impulse.

While *Coffee Grinds* expands with continuous metamorphoses—animals, clouds and other forces of nature changing shape as if there is no difference, no distance between human psyche and nature—the repetitive, almost reductive, image/ language of *Rosestrikes* implode, suggesting a counter-balancing restraint. *Rosestrikes* suggests that the chaotic, centrifugal expansion of man into nature—where subjectivity merges with objects around it—can not be sustained; but must be sublimated by separation—human and intellectual—by thought and loss. While *Coffee Grinds* is about innocence—though of a puckish, teasing sort—*Rosestrikes* is about experience when innocence/union is split into endless particles.

Nevertheless, typical of the *Poetry of Motion,* each section contains echoes of the other. Coffee grinds themselves are made of endless particles. On the other hand, while, underlying *Rosestrikes*, there is a love story of loss and separation, there is also the hint in the final poem "Rosebud" that the loss can be/is transcended by a greater love once the ego is smashed into smithereens, losing itself.

*Rosestrikes and Coffee Grinds* reveals the dialectic at the heart of Sufism, the endless struggle between forces of disintegration and chaos and of counterbalancing unity and love. They permeate the poem in exquisite equilibrium.

## IV. Love and *Rosestrikes*

While desire is eternal and unobstructed, love is only possible from a state of fallen grace—a consciousness of loss.

Love in *Rosestrikes* has three aspects, political, human and divine, each requiring violence resulting in loss or ego immolation to be fully realized. In the English version of the poem, they are loosely grouped under three different headings. The section "Rosestrikes" refers more to political or sexual love. In these poems images of a town or the self burning—suggesting war—are often yoked to graphic images of a sexual content, "A fire in the rose," "Bushrose" and "Windrose" creating such a sequence.[1] The second, the "Moody Love" section focuses on the end of a love affair, the affair already off its peak of perfect physical union and in the process of disintegration.

In "Rosebud" the protagonist, a young boy, destroys the perfect unity in nature denoted by a web of "alifs" (signs for infinity) describing frost ("frost is woven with straight lines, i.e., with alifs/ crossing each other. Manna pouring from above…") when he crushes the frost with the heel. The act implies both a thrill—almost of a sexual nature—and a trauma, its cause undefined but palpably there. The trauma is accompanied by a disintegration of the self, the speaker referring to himself doing the act in the third person, "Frost bitten,/ I, his innocent face/ in its most tormented form,[2] "…Stinging nettles are blooming in my heart./ A kid, as me, that is my heel, crushed/ the frost. Fragments of frost broke the weave/ In the heart, cut it loose."[3] Nevertheless, the poem ends with a suggestion that this traumatic alienation and violence may be the path to a greater vision. In other words, the poem ends by pointing to the beginning of the whole poem, to the *Coffee Grinds* section which embodies the perfect state of union, between the mind and the

---

[1] In an essay I wrote translating this section in 2006 "Insurrection and the Dreaded Beauty of Sufism: Ideas Towards a Fundamentalist Poetics" I pointed how the Turkish Sufism's focus on suffering and blood rather than dancing and wine as a path to ecstasy led to a poetry which reflected the Iraq War from the Iraqi side, both of the towns and houses burning and the psychology, the belief system of the suicide bomber. His/ her self-immolation is a Sufi political act, a sacrifice, leading to a greater love, union with God. (*Bombay Gin, Issue 32*, The Naropa Press, 2006, pp. 57/8.)

[2] "Rosebud" ("The walk")

[3] "Rosebud" ("The Rush")

world, which *Rosestrikes* in its fragmented obsessiveness is trying to reach back or point to:

As the rainbow pleases mankind,
so does, it seems, crushing frost.

Because the inside of frost is hollow, the sound it makes being crushed is interesting.
…

As if a piece of music.
Exactly like the crushing of a particularly thin glass.
Maybe of a crystal bone.[1]


V. Freedom in *Coffee Grinds* — Stations of Love

A mountain. Flying to the sky. (As in all fortunes, is this mountain *an inner distress*? Shouldn't words, as moving targets, in fortunes also have various meanings? And couldn't unknown words enrich the interpretation, therefore a fortune?

The mountain is flying to the sky, continuing to fly, leaving its main mass of land behind. But also know that that block of mother land also will not remain where it was—are themselves blocks which will continue to fly. As big pieces, as small pieces they will fly to the sky, there forming a mountain.

Mountain, in the sky. Even though their densities are different, only clouds may sustain their existence as mass. If so, what's this mountain which has rediscovered itself doing here?

*You* can tell me that. But it seems you're emptying your insides. And this, in the tongue of *our* coffee grinds, means an easing up. (Easing up block by block. If it happened all at once, it'd be like an

---

[1] "Rosebud" ("The Crush")

electro-shock. Because of that, this way is a good thing. Maybe also the pace has to do with your personality.)

With this passing of the mountain to the sky, as if you are also being reborn. Midway, between sky and earth. And as if with your rebirth a crescent is oozing out from your skirt and mowing the skirt of the mountain.

Along with a cat in silhouette and a pregnant pigeon (or is it malignant) flying to the sky.

Between sky and earth, or, seen another way, like the depths of the sea. Heavy, silent, or functioning among the noises of the depth of the sea, the migrating mountain, parcels of mountain, rocks, stones, the silhouette of the cat, the pregnant pigeon, *you* wearing a long gown, tiny fish, a crescent moon like the knife… you're in that sea.

Or seen from another angle…

The crescent is also on the saucer of the cup, in addition, exactly opposite the crescent inside the cup. Exactly like the reflection of a mirror, the right side on the left. The left, on the right, etc. (Or, to say more, the West in the east, the North south…)

According to looking in the mirror, hearts are on the right.

Does this alter anything, anything?

Opposite the crescent (the one in the saucer, that is crescent in the mirror) there is a *star*. (Like a flag, exactly!)

The crescent becoming a full moon, that star also will keep growing.

(Why the mountain is migrating to the sky is now crystal clear.)

Finito!)[1]

## VI. Translation Strategies

"Things do not connect; they correspond. That is what makes it possible for a poet to translate real objects, to bring them across language as clearly as he can bring them across time. That tree you saw in Spain is a tree I could never have seen in California, that lemon has a different smell and a different taste. BUT the answer is this—every place and every time has a real object to *correspond* with your real object—that lemon may become this lemon or it may even become this piece of seaweed, or in this particular color of gray in this ocean. One does not need to imagine that lemon; one needs to discover it.

Even these letters. They *correspond* with something. (I don't know what) that you have written (perhaps as unapparently as that lemon corresponds to this piece of seaweed) and, in turn, some future poet will write something which *corresponds* to them. That is how we dead men write to each other."[2]

The heart of *Coffee Grinds* is the crystalline purity of its movements, which project an almost perfect state of harmony between the subjective mind—projecting itself into the world, eliminating distance—and the world. The central image of the section is the mirror—the cup mirroring the sky, the coffee grounds the mind—its illusionary transparence. The poem consists of the traces the mind etches on this transparence, the mental calligraphy it creates. *Coffee Grinds* is a quintessential *Poetry of Motion* poem. Erözçelik's style in this section—his long, flat lines verging on but never quite becoming prose—creates the vehicle for the arabesque the language traces, its almost visual dimension.[3] Since motion—specifically *its shape*—is the essence of

[1] *Coffee Grinds* (#2)
[2] *After Lorca*, (*The Collected Books of Jack Spicer*, Black Sparrow Press, 1996, p. 34
[3] The sinuous, flat line, without the jump cuts, constitutes also the style of Lale Müldür's "Waking to Constantinople" and Enis Batur's "Passport." The line derives from the *Second New* poet İlhan Berk's "long line" which in many ways anticipates and opens the path to the

the poem—movement as essence—my purpose as a translator has been to preserve all the creases, darts, tugs, etc., the "awkward," ritualistic motions of the original in English, acting as a flow chart—a very precise one—of the original's cadences. The translation acts as a recorder/ recoder of that flow as time.

In *Rosestrikes*, Erözçelik's style looks back to the 1960's *Second New* poet Ece Ayhan, whose style involves exploring and exploiting multiple layering of words in puns, aural deconstructions, etc.[1] Instead of moving on a flat, visual surface, in *Rosestrikes* the poems progress *inside* words, the repetitive, obsessive echoes variant, multiple meanings of a given word create rubbing against each other.[2] *Rosestrikes* is built around a small group of word/ sound constellations. The basic three are: ay (moon, ah!)/aya (to the moon, holy), ayva (quince), ayı (the animal bear); gül (rose), gül (to smile). The third is built around a deconstruction of the word "kırağı" (frost). "Kır-" means "meadow," "to break," "to hurt"; "ağ" means "web, net," "to rise to the sky"; "ağı" means "poison."[3] "Rosebud," the penultimate poem in the book, is a narrative woven around the multiple meanings of a word, "a poem, but a cry inside one word." In fact, "Rosebud" is a narrative *into* the potential, buried meanings of the word "Kırağı," exploding them.[4]

The main challenge translating *Rosestrikes* is that the poetic center of the poem, its *Eda*, is totally sealed, in Walter Benjamin's words, in the specific "modes of intention[5]" of Turkish. The same three words in English are devoid of any mesh of aural associations. It is paradoxically this elusive otherness which elicits the almost erotic impulse to translate it, giving it,

<hr />

*Poetry of Motion*. (See *Eda*, "The Idea of A Book," pp.16/20; *Eda*, "Annotations on Lale Müldür's 'Waking to Constantinople,'" pp. 334/6.)

[1] See Ece Ayhan. *A Blind Cat Black and Orthodoxies* (Sun & Moon Press, 1997), to be reprinted by Green Integer Press in 2011.

[2] This is relatively easier to do in Turkish because of its narrow sound range due to vowel harmony. Vowels in Turkish are divided into narrow and open ones. If a word starts with an open vowel, or vice versa, as a general rule, the other vowels in the word must follow suit.

[3] Erozçelik had a book of poetry published in 1991 entitled *Kırağı*.

[4] The English version of "Rosebud" in *Rosestrikes* is preceded by two diagrams. one of them hand-drawn by Erozçelik showing the multiple meanings of the word "Kiragi." It appears that some of the hermetic, "sacred" meanings of Turkish—the poetic quality of *Eda* in it—can only be transferred into English visually, as space where chronological time and syntactic sequencing thins out into multiple directions.

[5] "The Task of the Translator," *Illuminations*, p. 74

again in Benjamin's words, "translatability.[1]" My solution was to search for possible corresponding verbal constellations in English. My central discovery turned out to be the group "hearth-heart-earth-death" which through its "fire" and "death" connotations creates a wormhole—a parallel verbal space—to the original poem, fire and burning being the engines of spiritual dissolution and rebirth in Turkish Sufism and in Erözçelik's poem.[2] Here, the four words generate their own space, parallel to but to some degree independent from the original. The second discovery was the pun between "leave" (belonging to plants) and "leave" (meaning departure and loss), with its own nexus of vegetal life and yearning. The third was the odd, dissonant correspondence between the flower "rose" and "rose" as the past tense of "to rise," as in "the moon rose." The rose and the moon consistently exchange places, as twin objects, in Erözçelik's poem in Turkish.

## V. Correspondence — The Reality of Jack Spicer's Real Objects

While the translation of *Telve/ Coffee Grinds* tries to achieve a partially visual perfect "faithfulness," as in a mirror, the translations in *Rosestrikes* often split the originals into fragments. This is necessary partly because due to its wider sound range it is much harder to sustain obsessive aural sequences in English, and the original must be diverted into two. What is more, the constellation of words in English—heart, hearth, earth, death, for instance—having its own dynamic energy, takes the original piece in its own direction, creating a number of meta-poems—not in the original, but spun out of them.[3] It is through the interactions among the meta poems and fragments that the corresponding parallel space of the poem in English is created. *Rosestrikes* looks at its original *Gül* distortedly, as if through a broken glass darkly.

---

[1] "The Task," pp. 78/9.

[2] I hit upon the possibility of this chain of connections after reading Simon Pettet's beautiful book *Hearth* (Talisman Books, 2008).

[3] Erözçelik's original *Gül* consists of twenty-three pieces. This number in *Rosestrikes* is forty-seven. Erözçelik himself considers number twenty-three significant. Adding to it one to represent *Rosestrikes and Coffee Grinds* as a whole, one reaches a number which matches the number of coffee grinds readings in the book. This numerological correspondence is lost in *Rosestrikes*.

One can look at a sequence of three poems in the book, "H-Rose," "Jamrose" and "Rosecandy," to get a sense of the process. The first is a meta-poem generated from the first three lines of the Turkish original. "Jamrose" is almost a perfect replication of that original poem. "Rosecandy" is, except for the last line, a quite faithful rewriting of a poem which appears three poems later in the original. It is the letter "h," popping out of the word "hearth" and sparking/sparkling as "the gibberish/ of the bursting hearth// exiled// to alchemical// dots," which seems to unify the space of the three poems, each looking separately/apart at a distance, as if "in a coma." The letter "h" is the real object, the "seaweed," corresponding to Spicer's "lemons" in the original.

Here lies the paradox of Erözçelik's *Gül* and of its translation *Rosestrikes*. *Rosestrikes* reflects the original in a splintered state. On the other hand, the original *Gül*, too, depicts states of loss—splintering from the state of oneness the earlier part *Coffee Grinds* embodies. It is a poem of experience. Every poem in *Gül* is about yearning, exile, the reaching back to the state of union with "the other" the Sufi *Arc of Descent* trying to transform itself into an *Arc of Ascent* expresses.[1] In a sense the fragmentation in *Rosestrikes* reflects what *Gül is*. The fragmentation of the original poem in the attempt to capture its obsessive style leads the translation to reveal in itself, though inadvertently, the very nature of what the original is: a reflection of separateness from a lost unified state. Every poem both in *Gül* and *Rosestrikes,* in fact *Rosestrikes and Coffee Grinds* as a whole, embody different states of yearning. In that way they represent the very essence of the Sufi experience: through the prism of multiplicity, disintegration and chaos to have a glimpse of a state of divine (Islamic or pagan) unity:

Swimrose

Magnetism
swimmingly

the rose
swimmingly

---

[1] To read more about the Sufi *Arcs of Descent and Ascent*, see "*souljam/ cangüncem*: küçük İskender's Subjectivity," *Eda*, pp. 339/41.

the sky swimmingly
the green swimmingly

...[1]

—*Murat Nemet-Nejat*

[1]*Rosestrikes*

**Seyhan Erözçelik** was born in 1962 in Bartın, a town in the Black Sea region of Turkey. He studied psychology at Boğaziçi University and oriental languages at Istanbul University. In 1986, he co-founded the Şiir Atı (Horse of Poetry) publishing house which published over forty titles in 1980s. He is a member of the Turkish Pen Center and Writer's Syndicate of Turkey. He lives in Istanbul.

His first poem "Düştanbul" (Dreamstanbul) was published in 1982, followed by a number of collections. He has also written poems in the Bartın dialect and in other Turkic languages, and has brought a modern approach to to the classical Ottoman rhyme, aruz, in his book *Kara Yazılı Meşkler* (Tunes Written on the Snow) (2003). He has published a critical essay on the modern mystical poet Âsaf Hâlet Çelebi, collected works of the forgotten poet Halit Asım, and translated the poetry of Osip Mandelstam and C. P. Cavafy into Turkish.

He was awarded the Yunus Nadi Prize in 1991, the Behçet Necatigil Poetry Prize in 2004 and the Dionysos Prize in 2005.

Publications: *Yeis ile Tabanca* (Despair and Pistol) (1986), *Hayal Kumpanyası* (The Troop of Imagination) 1990), *Kır Ağı* (Hoarfrost) (1991), *Gül ve Telve* (Rosestrikes and Coffee Grinds) (1997), *Şehirde Sansar Var!* (There is a Marten in Town!) (1999), *Kitap, bitti!* (The Book is Over!) (2003), *Kitaplar* (Books, collected poems) (2003), *Yağmur Taşı* (The Rainstone) (2004), *Vâridik, Yoğidik* (Once We Were, We Weren't) (2006).

Poet, translator and essayist, **Murat Nemet-Nejat**'s edited and largely translated *Eda: A Contemporary Anthology of Turkish Poetry* (2004), translated Orhan Veli, *I, Orhan Veli* (1989), Ece Ayhan, *A Blind Cat Black and Orthodoxies* (1997). He is the author of *The Peripheral Space of Photography* (2004) and, recently, the poems "I Did My Best Work During a Writer's Block" (2009), "Disappearances" (2010) and "Alphabet Dialogues/Penis Monologues" (2010). The poem *The Spiritual Life of Replicants* will be published soon. He is presently working on the long poem "The Structure of Escape."